Asphalt State Park

By Phil Frank

D0770414

Brinker, Ink. • Oakland, California

PUBLISHED IN THE UNITED STATES OF AMERICA
BY

OAKLAND, CALIFORNIA

ALL RIGHTS RESERVED.

Asphalt State Park

By

Phil Frank

ASPHALT STATE PARK, haven of the motorized camper, home of denatured wildlife, located in the Clearcut Mountains in an unrecorded section of the American wilderness, welcomes you.

Asphalt State Park is a slice of urban culture transported to the woods. It is a place of paved campsites, a gas station, 24 hour convenience store, cable TV hookups and morning paper deliveries. It is, in short, an oasis for the four-wheeled vagabonds of the urban environment.

Farley, a traveling newspaper reporter, stumbles upon the park amidst his wanderings around the country.

Because of his affinity for animals, Farley is recruited by Ranger Malone, the dictatorial head ranger, to deal with the park bears, a thorn in the head ranger's paw... so to speak.

Ranger Malone, a paper-shuffling bureaucrat who can't tell an eagle from a mealworm, on permanent assignment to Asphalt State Park, has taken it as his charge to "humanize" the wilderness by paving everything in sight.

A one-sided relationship blossomed early in Farley's career as a seasonal ranger when **Hilda**, a brown bear with a thing for uniforms, takes a shine to Farley. She was doomed to carry a torch forever for the man of her dreams and he in turn was doomed to be the object of the affections of a 500 pound relative of the grizzly.

By the time that Farley returned for his second summer, the pattern was set... the head ranger, living in fear of the animals running the park from his underground bunker, the park visitors running rampant in the woods while the bears reveled in the loot purloined from campers and became totally dependent upon these urban visitors for junk food, batteries and luxury items that were now a natural part of their habitat.

With the beginning of this new summer season a new character is added to the cast..., the daughter of chief-of-staff Malone. Ranger Loretta will occupy Fire Tower Five on the outer perimeter of Asphalt State Park, isolated by her father from the male staff members of the park. Somewhat aloof in her personality, it will take many visits to the foot of her fire tower for Farley to catch her eye. Shall we begin?

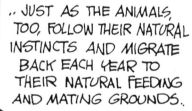

HOW ARE THE TRACKING DEVICES WORKING, GRABER?

GREAT, FARLEY.. I'M GETTING SHARP, CLEAR SIGNALS..

WELL, I'LL TELL YOU **THIS** MUCH.. I THINK IT'S A **DISGRACE** THAT THEY DRUGGED US AND FORCED US TO WEAR THESE RADIO DEVICES!!

HOLD STILL WHILE I ADJUST THIS THING.. ..**THERE**!

THE DRUGGING PART WASN'T SO BAD!

LISTEN, GRABER.. I COULD SWEAR I HEAR DISCO MUSIC..

OCCASIONALLY OUR BEARS WILL GET A BIT TOO ROWDY SO WE'LL PUT OUT SOME GARBAGE LACED WITH TRANQUILIZERS..

THEN WE'LL PICK UP THE BEARS AND DROP 'EM OFF SOME DISTANCE FROM THE CAMPSITES WHERE THEY WERE BECOMING A NUISANCE..

WOW.. THAT WAS **SOME** PARTY LAST NIGHT!

YEAH.. WONDER WHAT WAS IN THAT GARBAGE..

SAY.. JUST WHERE **ARE** WE, ANYWAY?

OH.. OH..

CITY LIMITS TIJUANA

SIR.. THE BEARS HAVE BROKEN ALL THE CEMENT FORMS FOR THE CURBS IN THE WILDERNESS AREA..

..AND MY TRAFFIC LIGHTS?

FARLEY IS A FINK.

PAVE PARADISE???

THE BEARS TOOK THEM TO DECORATE THEIR NIGHTCLUB..

HEATHENS! THEY CAN'T STOP PROGRESS.

PASS THE WORD.. WE POUR AT MIDNIGHT!

WORDS THAT WILL LIVE IN INFAMY..

WHAT YOU DOING, FARLEY?

I'M TAGGING ALL THE VEGETATION, FLOYD..

MOST OF THE VISITORS TO OUR PARK ARE FROM THE BIG CITIES, FLOYD. A LOT OF NATURE IS NEW TO THEM..

..SO, THE HEAD RANGER MADE UP THESE TAGS TO HELP EDUCATE THE PUBLIC.

TREE.

GOOD MORNING, CAMPERS.. AND WELCOME TO ASPHALT STATE PARK THIS **LABOR DAY** WEEKEND..

WE'RE PLANNING ANOTHER '**NATURE DAY**' ON SATURDAY WHICH WILL INCLUDE A **MANDATORY** 18-MILE NATURE HIKE.. A **VEGETARIAN** POTLUCK.. ..NO VEHICLES OR ALCOHOLIC BEVERAGES BEING ALLOWED IN THE PARK.. THE HEAD RANGER WILL GIVE A TALK ENTITLED "**WOOD TICKS OF THE NORTHWEST**".

..FOLLOWED BY THE ANNUAL BURNING OF THE RANGER STATION..

BEAUTIFUL PHOTO FOR YOUR ALBUM.. ..OKAY, SMILE.. **GOT IT!**

click

THANKS FOR VISITING **ASPHALT STATE PARK**

'BYE! SEE YOU NEXT YEAR.

HMM.. THE HENDERSONS ARE BACKING UP..

OUR CAMERA, PLEASE.

A-HEM!

THE NIGHT IS STILL. THE STARS SHINE LIKE PINHOLES IN THE BLACK CURTAIN OF SPACE.

THE LONELY FIGURE OF A RANGER PICKS HIS WAY THROUGH THE SILENT LANDSCAPE OF THE NIGHT WORLD, A SINGULAR PURPOSE ON HIS MIND...

UNABLE TO SLEEP, HE HAS ONCE AGAIN SOUGHT OUT THE CONFUSING AND MYSTERIOUS FIGURES...
... AND AGAIN THE BURNING QUESTION ARISES..

HOW COULD I LOSE FIFTEEN PICNIC TABLES?!

THE seasons have changed and with the last snow melting the Seasonal Ranger has returned.. ...but this year the friendly bears are not so friendly. The tedium of the wilderness experience is weighing heavy on their hairy shoulders.

They are under under pressure by management to perform for visitors... posing for candid roadside photos, fishing in Asphalt Creek or romping merrily in the clover filled meadows. Work hours have increased and rumblings are heard amongst the pines.

For the first time in the history of the park system there is talk amongst the animals... of a strike!

I REALIZE THE BEARS ARE AN IMPORTANT PART OF **ASPHALT STATE PARK**'S IMAGE.. ..BUT LET'S FACE IT..

..THEY'RE NOTHING BUT TROUBLE — WITH A CAPITAL **T**!

THEY'RE LAZY, UNRULY, UNKEMPT HEATHENS WHO SCAM AND PILFER AND PARTY ALL NIGHT!

I'VE BEEN IN TOUCH WITH A PROFESSIONAL BEAR TRAINER...

I'M THINKING OF HAVING OUR BEARS PROVIDED BY A PRIVATE CONTRACTOR..

RANGER MALONE IS PLANNING TO REPLACE THE WILD BEARS OF **ASPHALT STATE PARK** WITH TRAINED CIRCUS BEARS.. IN DESPERATION THE BEARS SEND A SPY TO GET INFORMATION FROM ONE OF THE RANGERS..

PSSST!! FARLEY!

RANGER FARLEY

WHO IS IT?

IT IS I, 'MATA HAIRY'..

SORRY, I COULDN'T RESIST THAT ONE..

DEAR RANGER MALONE.. THIS MORNING ONE OF THE BEARS' UNION OFFICIALS RAN OFF WITH THEIR PENSION FUNDS..

..THE RECENT UNIONIZATION OF THE BEARS HAS BEEN MORE THAN I CAN BEAR TAKE. I NEED SOME PEACE AND QUIET..

..I'VE GONE INTO THE WOODS FOR A FEW DAYS TO CLEAR MY MIND.. ATTACHED PLEASE FIND THE KEY TO THE ROOT CELLAR..

..YOU MAY WANT TO LOCK YOURSELF INTO IT UNTIL I GET BACK.
GOOD LUCK, FARLEY

PHIL FRANK

WHICH WAY IS IT BACK TO ASPHALT STATE PARK?

GOT ME..

WE'VE BEEN GOING IN CIRCLES FOR HOURS..

GREAT! WE CAN'T FIND FARLEY AND NOW WE'RE LOST..

THIS'LL MAKE GREAT HEADLINES..

PHIL FRANK

"FOUR BEARS LOST IN THE WOODS!!"

HOW EMBARRASSING..

CHIEF, THE SEARCH CREW HAS TURNED UP NO SIGN OF **FARLEY**, BUT WE DID FIND THE 4 BEARS WHO WENT LOOKING FOR HIM..

THE BEARS MADE THEIR WAY TO A ROAD. WE PICKED THEM UP AT A RESTAURANT **20** MILES SOUTH OF HERE..

GREAT!! JUST WAIT'LL MY SUPERIORS HEAR ABOUT THIS... ..IT'S GOING TO COST ME..

BEAR RAID SIREN

PHIL FRANK

SPEAKING OF COSTS.. THEIR DINNER CAME TO $34.50 INCLUDING THE TIP..

LOOK, SIR.. YOU'VE GOT A DAUGHTER IN A FIRE TOWER IN SECTOR 4, RIGHT?

RIGHT.

..AND THERE'S THIS LONELY RANGER **FARLEY** WANDERING AROUND IN THE **SAME** SECTOR, RIGHT?

RIGHT.

PHIL (IT LOOKS LIKE RAIN) FRANK

.. AND YOU'RE WORRIED HE'S CARRYIN' A TORCH FOR YOUR DAUGHTER, RIGHT?

RIGHT..

.. AND YOU'VE GOT FOUR AIR-TANKER PLANES ON THE RUNWAY FILLED WITH COLD WATER, RIGHT?

YOU'RE SICK.

THIS IS YOUR DAUGHTER **LORETTA** CALLING.. I KNOW YOU'RE THERE.. I CAN HEAR YOU CHUCKLING..

8-17

RANGER **FARLEY** AND I WERE JUST DOUSED BY FOUR AIR TANKER LOADS OF COLD WATER!

BUT I'M JUST CON- CERNED ABOUT YOUR WELL-BEING..

NEXT TIME I'M ON A DATE, DADDY...

..AND NEED AIR SUPPORT, **I'LL** CALL **YOU!**

I JUST WANTED A FEW DAYS ALONE IN THE WOODS.. IT DIDN'T SEEM LIKE A LOT TO ASK..

WELCOME **ASPHALT STATE PARK**

I WAS FOLLOWED BY BEARS.. STRAFED BY TANKER PLANES FULL OF FIRE RETARDANT..

..TOSSED OUT OF A FIRE TOWER BY A LADY RANGER, AND ..RUN OVER BY A DEPARTMENT OF THE INTERIOR OFFICIAL ON A DIRT BIKE..

LAUNDROMAT

.. AT LEAST I STILL HAVE THE PRIVACY OF MY OWN TENT..

I'LL SEE YOU.. AND RAISE YOU $5..

I'M OUT..

As long as visitors have been coming to the wilderness, they have been humbled by the majesty of nature. They sit transfixed by the late night starlit skies framed by majestic evergreens and stare intently into the embers of a campfire at midnight and ask themselves the eternal question: "Where can I get a candybar at this hour?"

That question will at last be answered. The park has awarded a contract for a 24 hour convenience store....

OKAY! I'M SICK AND TIRED OF WAKING UP EVERY MORNING TO A NEWSPAPER HITTING MY DOOR!

ONE MORE TIME AND IT'LL BE THE LAST TIME YOU DELIVER A NEWSPAPER IN _THIS_ STATE PARK!!

SLAM!

JEESH! WHAT A GROUCH.

ATTENTION, CAMPERS!! THE NATURE HIKE WILL LEAVE IN FIVE MINUTES..

MAKE SURE YOU HAVE YOUR LUNCH PACKS..

MRS. VELCRO.. IT'S ABOUT YOUR SHOES..

I KNOW. I JUST COULDN'T DECIDE..

..WHETHER TO WEAR MY BEACH THONGS FOR CASUAL STROLLING OR MY 'WAFFLE STOMPERS' FOR MOUNTAINOUS COUNTRY...

SO YOU WORE ONE OF EACH.

RIGHT ON, RANGER.

I t is spring. The bears are rising from their winter hibernation, having put in a wake up call for May. Park visitors are changing the oil in their motorhomes in preparation for another forage into the wilderness and the Seasonal Ranger sets aside his journalistic duties and dons his uniform for his return to Asphalt State Park. This season he brings with him a new character... ...a streetwise, loud-mouthed raven named Bruce. Raised in captivity and fed on fresh deli pastrami, Bruce is reluctant to leave the security of his urban environment for the mysteries of the woods.

You **EAT** these things?

PHIL (ONCE UPON A GREAT NATION.) FRANK

PHIL (WHAT'S MAYAN IS YOURS.) FRANK

A LONELY FIGURE STANDS AT THE CABIN WINDOW.. A BIRD SITS IN ITS CAGED, DEJECTED..

LORETTA..

IN A TOWER FAR AWAY A FIRE SPOTTER STARES LONGINGLY INTO THE DISTANCE.. ISOLATED BY HER SCOUNDREL FATHER..

SIGH..

BACK IN HIS CABIN THE RANGER GAZES LISTLESSLY INTO HIS COFFEE, AWARE THAT IT IS IMPOSSIBLE FOR HIM TO REACH OUT TO HIS TRUE LOVE..

PHIL C. (PREPARE FOR DEPARTURE) FRANK

.."FOR SHE IS ISOLATED A GREAT DISTANCE AWAY.. .. FIVE MILES AS THE CROW FLIES..

AS THE CROW FLIES?

I WON'T DO IT!

OUR STORY AT THE MOMENT: MRS. MELMAC, STRIPPED OF HER INDUSTRIAL INSECT KILLER, ARMED ONLY WITH A CAN OF **RAID**, AWAITS HER FATE..

COME AND GET ME!

ASPHALT STATE PARK

THE CRY OF A RAVEN CARRYING A MESSAGE OF LOVE FROM RANGER FARLEY TO RANGER LORETTA IN HER FIRE TOWER CAN BE HEARD ACROSS THE HILLS..

WHERE AM I?

TWO OF THE PARK BEARS, HAVING RECENTLY PURCHASED A MINING LEASE, ARE TUNNELING UNDER THE PARK IN SEARCH OF A RARE MINERAL..

AND THE HEAD RANGER HAS JUST MADE THE WEEK'S ASSIGNMENTS..

JUNIOR WEASELS NATURE HIKE..

NO!! NO!! PLEASE!!

PHIL (GREEN ACHERS) FRANK

REMEMBER THESE IMPORTANT FACTS.

THERE'LL BE A QUIZ ON TUESDAY.

While I nodded, nearly napping, suddenly there came a tapping..

..as of someone gently rapping.. ..rapping at the cabin floor..

TAP!! TAP!!

..cabin **FLOOR?**

BANG!! BANG!! CRACK!!

BEAR!!

WHERE?

LET ME SEE THAT MAP!

PHIL (JUST ATTIC WIT.)FRANK

LET ME SEE THIS MINERAL LEASE YOU BOUGHT.

HERE.

THIS IS A 1977 RENTAL AGREEMENT FOR A FLAT IN **TEANECK, NEW JERSEY!**

IT DOESN'T SAY ANYTHING ABOUT **UNOBTAINIUM?**

THERE **IS** NO SUCH THING AS UNOBTAINIUM.

MAYBE **THAT'S** WHY IT'S SO HARD TO FIND.

PHIL (SPARE NO EXPENSE!) FRANK

I'M SURPRISED THIS DOESN'T INCLUDE A LEASE TO THE BROOKLYN BRIDGE.

ARE YOU KIDDING? THAT ONE WAS **WAY** TOO EXPENSIVE.

SO.. JUNIOR WEASELS.. TELL US WHAT BROUGHT YOU TO **ASPHALT STATE PARK**?

MY NAME'S **RODNEY**..

MY FAMILY'S BEEN KICKED OUT OF FOUR PARKS ALREADY THIS SUMMER FOR RIDING OUR DIRT BIKES THROUGH THE BATHROOMS.

I'M **RICO**.. I'M ON CAMP FURLOUGH FROM THE **MODOC JUVENILE HOME** WHERE I'M DOING TWO YEARS FOR AGGRAVATED GRAFFITI ON A BUS DRIVER.

PAUL (TIME ON FOR BAD BEHAVIOR) FRANK

I'M **PHILLIPA**.. MY PARENTS DROPPED ME AT THE FRONT GATE AND SAID "WELCOME TO CAMP **RESTOFYOURLIFE**".

OKAY, **JUNIOR WEASELS**.. LET'S ASSUME WE'RE LOST IN THE WOODS..

NO FOOD.. NO WATER.. YOU'RE UNFAMILIAR WITH THE TERRAIN.. WHAT'S THE FIRST THING YOU DO?

YES, **RICO**..

PAUL (LIVE FREE OR PINE OUT..) FRANK

FIND THE NEAREST SNACK DISPENSER AND RIP THE FRONT OFF IT.

Panel 1: OH OH.. RANGER **FARLEY** HAS A BAD BUG BITE. WHAT **JUNIOR WEASEL** KNOWS WHAT TO DO?

I DO. I DO.

Panel 2: HERE, RANGER... PICK THIS PLANT AND RUB IT ON THE BITE..

OKAY, PHILIPPA.

Panel 3: INDIANS BELIEVED THAT BY RUBBING THIS PLANT ON IT YOU'D SOON FORGET ALL ABOUT YOUR INSECT BITE..

AND WHY'S THAT, PHILIPPA?

Panel 4: BECAUSE IT'S POISON IVY.

PHIL (COME UP AND SEE MY ITCHINGS.) FRANK

Panel 5: LORETTA.. IT'S BEEN SO LONG..

TOO LONG, FARLEY..

Panel 6: LORETTA..

YES, FARLEY?

Panel 7: BEFORE WE GET UNDER WAY WE ASK YOU ALL TO PLEASE RISE..

PRESS

GO FARLEY!

LORETTA

PHIL (WE ARE NOT ALONE, RANGER.) FRANK

Panel 8: OH, SAY, CAN YOU SEE.. BY THE DAWN'S EARLY LIGHT..

YOU COULD HAVE COME TO SEE **ME** TOO, **LORETTA!**

YOU **KNOW** I'M REQUIRED TO STAY IN THIS TOWER..

UP IN YOUR **IVORY** TOWER, IF I MIGHT ADD!! OH, AND BY THE WAY.. IT HAPPENS TO BE **296** STEPS UP TO SEE YOU.. NOT **293!**

COUNT 'EM AGAIN ON YOUR WAY DOWN!

WATCH OUT FOR THAT FIRST STEP. IT'S A BIG ONE.

PHIL (I'VE LOST MY VERTICAL HOLD.) FRANK

OOO! THAT WAS QUITE A SHOT TO **FARLEY'S** .. ER.. EGO.

WELL, WHAT DID YOU THINK OF THAT ACTION, **HOWARD?**

WELL, **FLOYD..** IT WAS A CLASSIC BATTLE OF THE SEXES..

PRESS

LORETTA WAS JUST GREAT.. SHE'S OBVIOUSLY BEEN TRAINING HARD..

WHEN SHE THREW THAT FIRST JAB AT **FARLEY** THE WRITING WAS ON THE WALL..

HIS FEEBLE ATTEMPTS TO JUSTIFY HIS EXISTENCE WERE MET WITH STRONG REBUTTAL.

IT WAS ALL OVER IN A MATTER OF MOMENTS..

PHIL (A GLITCH ON THE VIDEOSCREEN OF LIFE) FINK

THANK YOU, **HOWARD.**

ANY TIME, **FLOYD.**

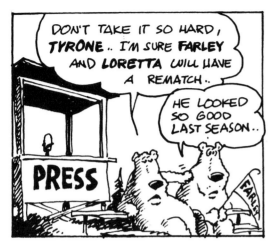

YOU KNOW.. I FEEL PRETTY BAD.. WE WERE PARTLY TO BLAME FOR FARLEY AND LORETTA'S BIG ARGUMENT.

SO?

I THINK WE SHOULD GET THEM BACK TOGETHER SOMEHOW.. LET'S ARRANGE A DINNER AT ALPHONSE'S PLACE..

HMM..

I'LL INVITE FARLEY.. YOU INVITE LORETTA. NEITHER WILL KNOW THE OTHER IS COMING.

IT SOUNDS TOTALLY UNDERHANDED, CONNIVING AND DECEITFUL!

I'LL DO IT.

PHIL (THE PLOT SICKENS.) FRANK

THE PITCH IS ON THE WAY..

THIS RELATIONSHIP WITH LORETTA HAS GONE ON A LONG TIME.. PERHAPS TOO LONG..

ALL THE MORE REASON TO RESOLVE THE PROBLEM.

"IS NOT OLD WINE WHOLESOMEST, OLD PIPPINS TOOTHSOMEST, OLD WOOD BURN BRIGHTEST, OLD LINEN WASH WHITEST? OLD SOLDIERS, SWEET-HEARTS, ARE SUREST..

.. AND OLD LOVERS ARE SOUNDEST."

I REST MY CASE.

CLAP! CLAP!! CLAP!!

PHIL (THE PINENUT GALLERY) FRANK

THANK YOU.. THANK YOU..

CLAP! CLAP!

CLAP! CLAP!

Working at night behind locked doors, the journalist/seasonal ranger works on a major exposé of Asphalt State Park...

...from unionized wildlife to kickbacks on tranquilizers... from paved wilderness trails to campers who pilfer entire buildings...
...from an insensitive park administrator who runs the public campground like a private fiefdom to animal life so dependent on human contact that airdrops of food scraps are required during off-season months..

AND THE BEARS, SIR?

YES. WELL, THEY WILL FALL UNDER YOUR COMMAND AGAIN, **FARLEY**..

AND HOW HAVE THEY BEEN, SIR?

QUIET.. NO PROBLEM AT ALL FOR THE LAST SIX MONTHS..

AND TO WHAT DO YOU ATTRIBUTE **THAT**, SIR?

THEY'VE BEEN **ASLEEP**, YOU NINNY!!

FARL(WE'VE STRUCK LOGIC!)FRANK—

ISN'T IT DANGEROUS.. RELYING ON A COMPUTER TO HANDLE ALL THE PARK'S RECORDS?

NONSENSE!

THERE'S A SPECIAL ACCESS CODE KNOWN ONLY TO ME.. **I** ALONE CAN ORDER SUPPLIES..

..**NO ONE ELSE**!! NOT ANY RANGERS, WORKERS OR THOSE HEATHEN BEARS CAN..

KNOCK! KNOCK!

FARL(NO CRACKERS?)FRANK

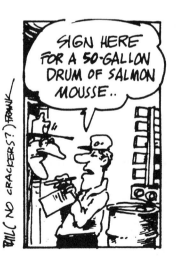

SIGN HERE FOR A 50-GALLON DRUM OF SALMON MOUSSE..

PHIL (LET'S GO TO THE MOVIES!) FRANK

PHIL (NATURE IGNORES A VACUUM.) FRANK

UNBEKNOWNST TO OUR UNDERCOVER REPORTER, THE HEAD RANGER HAS TAKEN A FREE ONE-MONTH SUBSCRIPTION TO THE **DAILY DEMISE**..

THUMP!

HIS EYE IS CAUGHT BY A HEADLINE: "CORRUPTION IN OUR PARK SYSTEM!!"

HMM..

"THE ADMINISTRATOR OF THIS PAVED WILDERNESS AREA IS A BEAK-NOSED, BORN-AGAIN BUREAUCRAT WHO RUNS THE PARK FROM HIS SHEETROCKED BUNKER."

GEE.. I LOVE SUCCESS STORIES..

WITH GREAT TREPIDATION **FARLEY** ENTERS RANGER **MALONE'S** BUNKER.. KNOWING FULL WELL HIS BOSS HAS SEEN A COPY OF **FARLEY'S** EXPOSÉ.

HELLO?

ENTER!

HAVE YOU SEEN THIS STORY IN THE DAILY DEMISE?
"IRON-FISTED ADMINISTRATOR"
".. PROTEGÉ OF JAMES WATT"
" PAVED WILDERNESS AREA"
"CHAUFFEURED LIMOUSINE"

WHAT I WANT TO KNOW IS..

..WHY CAN'T WE GET THIS KIND OF PRESS?

WELL?

PHIL (WITH A NAME LIKE SMUCKERS..) FRANK

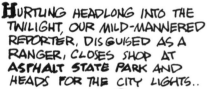

About the cartoonist...

Phil Frank has been putting pen to paper to tickle readers' funnybones since 1961 when he got his start at the Michigan State daily newspaper.

Since then millions have enjoyed his humorous illustration on posters, books, T-shirts, greeting cards, and most notably his two dailies - **Farley**, an exclusive *San Francisco Chronicle* comic feature, and **Miles to Go**, the nationally syndicated strip.

Asphalt State Park is a collection inspired by Phil's close association with naturalists of State Parks such as California's Yosemite. "I've always been struck by the ingenuity of bears to adapt to whatever way humans come up with to keep them away from food or out of the trash."

Phil and his wife Susan are long-time residents of Sausalito, California, and are active participants in community affairs. Phil rows to his studio, a pilot-house on an ancient ferryboat anchored among houseboats. This 10-foot-square studio houses among his cartooning books and research materials, noted collectables such as a stuffed raven and a telescope - with which he keeps a close eye on the sea life, and the neighbors.